The Nature Kid's Guide to
POLAR BEARS

DAVID ANDERSON

LP Media Inc. Publishing
Text copyright © 2026 by LP Media Inc.
All rights reserved.

For information address LP Media Inc. Publishing,
30012 Variolite St NW, Princeton MN 55371
www.lpmedia.org

Publication Data

Polar Bears
The Nature Kid's Guide to Polar Bears — First edition.

Summary: "Learn all about Polar Bears, the Nature Kid Way"
— Provided by publisher.

ISBN: 979-8-89818-175-8

[1. Polar Bears – Non-Fiction] I. Title.

Title: The Nature Kid's Guide to Polar Bears

CONTENTS

FROZEN HOME

Crunch! A polar bear walks across a sheet of bright white ice.

Polar bears live in the **Arctic**. It is one of the coldest places on Earth. Snow and ice stretch out as far as you can see.

Harsh winds whip across the land. Water freezes into thick sheets of sea ice. It gets so cold that your breath would freeze in the air!

But polar bears love it here. The cold does not bother them one bit. This frozen world is the perfect home.

DID YOU KNOW? In the Arctic winter, the sun does not rise for months at a time!

ARCTIC ADDRESS

Canada is home to more polar bears than any other country on Earth.

Whoosh! A polar bear trots across the snowy top of the world.

Far to the north, polar bears roam across icy lands. You can find them in Canada, Russia, and Norway. The only US state that is cold enough for them is Alaska!

Most polar bears stay close to the coast. They follow the sea ice as it shifts and moves. The ice helps them find food.

No polar bears live at the South Pole. That is penguin land! Look at the top of a globe, that is where you will find polar bear country.

BIGGEST BEARS

Thud! A giant polar bear drops down on all four paws.

Polar bears are the biggest bears in the world. A male polar bear can weigh more than 1,000 pounds. That is almost as heavy as some cars!

If a polar bear stands on its back legs it is almost as tall as a basketball hoop!

Female polar bears are smaller than males. But even a female polar bear is very big. She still weighs more than most other bears on Earth.

A polar bear paw can be about 12 inches wide. That is as big as a dinner plate!

BUILT TOUGH

Polar bear fur is not really white. Their hair is actually clear and hollow!

Brrr! The cold arctic wind howls, but the tough polar bear does not even shiver.

Polar bears are built for the cold. Under their skin is a thick layer of fat called **blubber**. It keeps them warm like a cozy coat.

Their fur has two layers. The outer hairs are long and oily. Water rolls right off. Below is soft, thick fur close to the skin. This fur traps in their body heat keeping them warm even in the coldest weather.

Under all that fur, polar bear skin is black. The dark color soaks up heat from the sun. This helps them stay warm even more.

SUPER SNIFFERS

Sniff, sniff! A polar bear lifts its nose to the icy wind.

A polar bear's nose is amazing. It can smell a seal from more than a mile away. That is like smelling lunch from across your town!

Polar bears can also see well in bright snow and dim light. Their small ears pick up sounds from far away. All three senses help them find food.

But smell is their true super power. A bear holds its nose high in the wind. One good sniff tells it which direction the seals are.

SNOW STEALTH

Shh! A polar bear blends into the snowy white land around it.

A polar bear's fur helps it hide in the snow. Against the bright ice, a bear is hard to spot. This is called **camouflage**.

Camouflage helps polar bears sneak up on prey. A seal may not see the bear until it is very close. The bear blends right in!

Their big size also keeps them safe. No animal ever attacks a full grown polar bear. No one wants to face those sharp teeth and claws!

Polar bears sometimes cover their black nose with a paw while hunting. Scientists think this may help them hide the one dark spot on their whole body!

SEAL
SNACKS

Chomp! A polar bear eats a big meal on the frozen sea ice.

Seals are the main food for polar bears. Ringed seals are their top pick. The fat in seals has lots of energy to help the bears stay big and warm.

Bears also eat other things when seals are hard to find. They munch on bird eggs, berries, and even seaweed.

In summer, food can be **scarce**. Bears may go weeks without a big meal. They live off the fat stored in their body.

A polar bear can eat up to 100 pounds of food in just one meal!

PATIENT POUNCE

Crack! A seal pops up through a hole, and the bear strikes fast.

Polar bears hunt with great patience. They find a hole in the sea ice. Seals come up through these holes to breathe.

The bear waits. It can stand still for hours! When a seal pops its head up for air — pounce! The bear grabs it with one fast swipe.

Bears also sneak up on seals resting on the ice. They creep low and slow. Then they charge!

Polar bears catch their meal in only about one out of every five hunts!

TOP DOG

Huge! A polar bear stands tall. It is the king of the Arctic.

No animal in the Arctic is tougher than a polar bear. It sits at the very top of the food chain. This makes it the top predator.

No animals would dare fight a polar bear. A walrus might use its big tusks to fight back. But most animals stay far away.

So what is a polar bear's biggest challenge? It is not another animal. It is finding enough food on the changing ice.

Arctic wolves sometimes steal scraps of food from a polar bear's meal!

STAY SAFE

DID YOU KNOW?
One polar bear was tracked
swimming 426 miles over nine
days!

Splash! A polar bear plunges through thin ice into cold water.

Even the biggest bears face dangers. As the Arctic warms, sea ice is breaking apart and melting earlier each year. This means polar bears sometimes have to swim very long distances to find solid ice for hunting.

Polar bears are strong swimmers, but even they can get tired. Cubs are especially at risk on long swims through cold, rough water.

When a bad storm hits, a polar bear digs a pit in the snow. It curls up and lets the snow pile on top like a blanket. The snow traps the bear's body heat and keeps it warm and safe until the storm passes.

GRIP STRONG

In the summer time polar bears sometimes slide down snowy hills on their bellies to cool off!
FUN FACT!

Crunch! Huge paws grip the ice as it walks across a frozen ridge.

We already know polar bears are champion swimmers, but they are just as impressive on land. Their huge paws act like snowshoes, spreading their weight across thin ice and soft snow so they do not sink in.

Those big paws also have rough, bumpy pads that grip slippery ice like football cleats. Sharp claws dig in with every step, keeping the bear steady on steep, frozen slopes.

Polar bears can sprint up to 25 miles per hour to chase prey. But most of the time, they walk with a slow, swaying shuffle to save energy between meals.

DAY BY DAY

Yawn! A polar bear stretches out on the ice after a long nap.

Polar bears spend a lot of their day resting. After a big meal, they may sleep for hours. Rest helps them save their strength.

When they are not sleeping, bears walk and look for food. They may wander for miles each day. A bear is always on the move.

Polar bears also like to play! They roll in the snow and toss chunks of ice. They keep clean by rubbing their fur in the snow.

A polar bear can nap anywhere, even on a floating chunk of sea ice!

LONE ROAMERS

Hush! A polar bear walks alone across the empty white ice.

Polar bears like to be alone. They do not live in packs or herds. Each bear roams the ice by itself.

Sometimes bears do meet up. If there is a lot of food in one spot, many bears may gather. They eat near each other but keep their space.

Young bears may play and wrestle. But once they grow up, they go their own way. A polar bear's life is mostly quiet and solo.

Groups of up to 40 polar bears have been spotted eating at one spot!

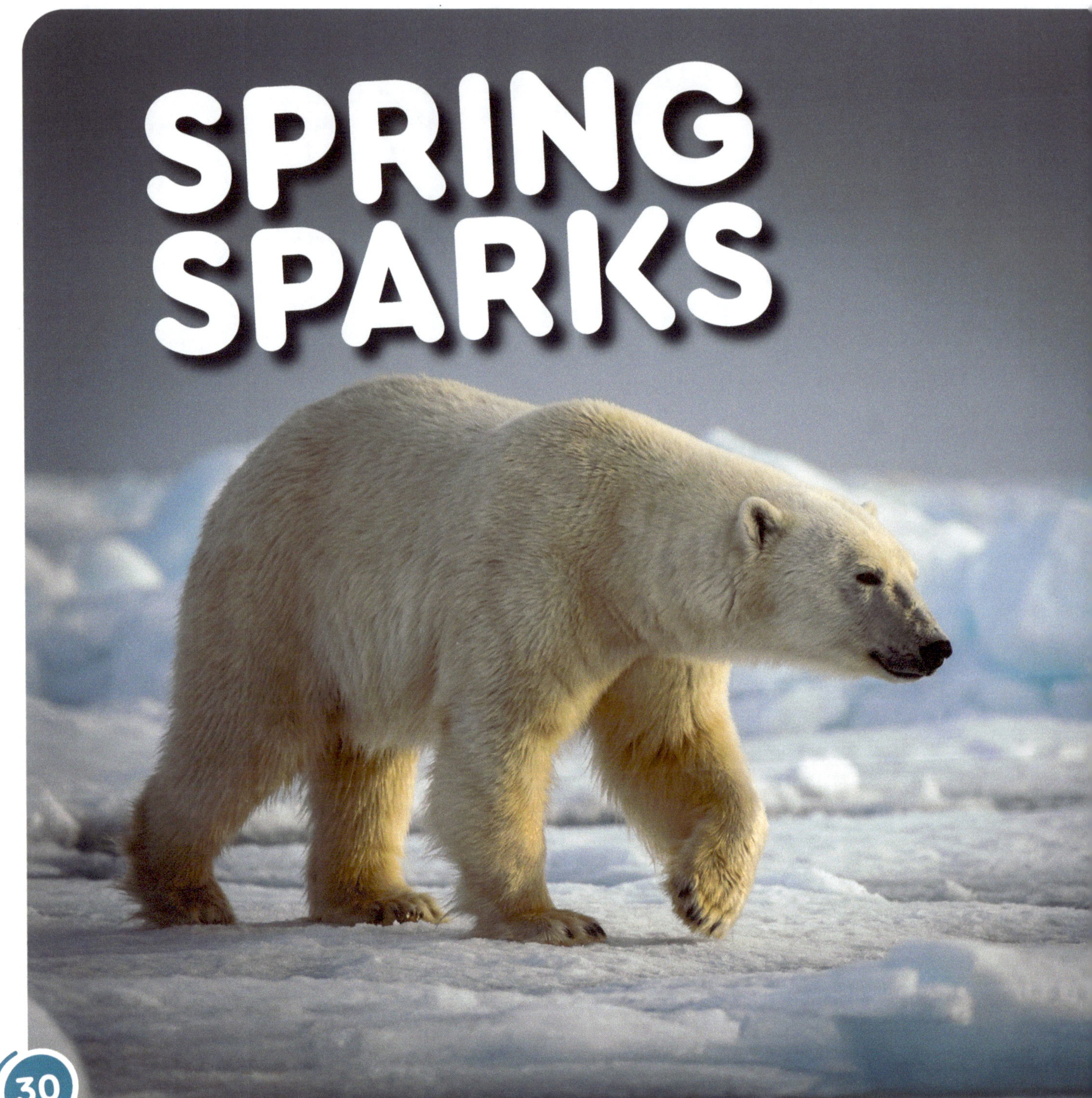
SPRING
SPARKS

Grunt! A male polar bear follows a scent trail across the ice.

Polar bears find mates in the spring. Males follow the scent of a female across the ice. They may travel a long way to find her.

When two males want the same female, they may fight. They push and shove with their big bodies. The winner gets to stay.

After mating, the male goes away. The female is on her own. She will soon need to get ready for cubs.

Polar bear pairs may stay together for only a few days, or up to two weeks!

CUDDLY CUBS

DID YOU KNOW?
A polar bear mother does not eat or drink for up to eight months while she is in the den caring for her cubs!

Squeak! Tiny polar bear cubs cry out in their snowy den.

Polar bear cubs are born in winter inside a snowy **den**. They weigh only about one pound, no bigger than a guinea pig! They are blind, toothless, and completely helpless.

The mother keeps them warm with her body and feeds them rich, fatty milk. The cubs grow so fast that by the time spring arrives, they are fluffy, round, and ready to explore.

Most mothers have two cubs. After about three months in the den, the little family steps outside together. For the cubs, it is their very first look at the frozen world they call home!

MAMA BEARS

Growl! A mother polar bear warns others to stay away from her cubs.

Mother polar bears work hard to keep their cubs safe. They stay with their young for about two years. Longer than most other animals!

Moms teach cubs how to hunt and swim. The little bears watch and copy what she does. Step by step, they learn to survive.

If danger comes near, the mother stands her ground. She will fight to protect her babies. No animal wants to face an angry mama bear!

Polar bear moms may lose half their body weight while caring for cubs!

MELTING ICE

Drip! A polar bear watches as the sea ice melts beneath its paws.

Polar bears are in trouble. The Earth is getting warmer, and the sea ice is melting. Bears need that ice to hunt for seals.

When the ice melts too early, bears must wait on land. There is less food to eat on shore. Some bears go hungry for a long time.

Pollution and oil spills also hurt bears. Dirty water can make them sick. The Arctic is changing fast, and bears need our help.

The Arctic is warming about two times faster than the rest of Earth!

HELPING
HANDS

Click! A polar bear wakes up. It just had a tracker put on!

People all over the world want to help polar bears. Scientists study them to learn what they need. They track bears with special collars.

Many countries have laws to protect polar bears. Some places set aside safe land just for wildlife. This helps keep bears safe.

Zoos and wildlife centers raise orphaned cubs and teach people why polar bears matter. The more we learn about these amazing animals, the better we can protect them.

There are only about 26,000 polar bears left in the wild right now!

GLOSSARY

Arctic
The very cold region near the North Pole

blubber
A thick layer of fat under a polar bear's skin

camouflage
Colors or patterns that help an animal blend in and hide

scarce
Hard to find because there is not very much of it.

den
A sheltered spot where an animal rests or has babies